101 Shaggy Dog Stories
by E. RICHARD & LINDA R. CHURCHILL
Cartoons by HOWARD KATZ

SCHOLASTIC INC.
New York Toronto London Auckland Sydney

ISBN 0-590-40412-1

12 11 10 9 8 7 6   4 5 6 7 8 9/9

What is worse than a shaggy dog
howling at the moon?

> *Two shaggy dogs howling at the
> moon.*

Which dog tastes best when eaten?

A hot dog.

Which dog is always without a tail?

A hot dog.

•

Which dog eats with its tail?

All dogs keep their tails on when eating.

Why wasn't the shaggy dog hurt when
he fell off a 100-foot ladder?

He fell from the bottom rung.

What time is it when your shaggy watchdog lets a robber take the family silver?

Time to get a new watchdog.

What would you get if you crossed a chicken with a shaggy dog?

A hen that lays pooched eggs.

How do you make a shaggy dog float?

Take two scoops of ice cream, a couple of squirts of soda, and a small shaggy dog.

What was the shaggy dog doing on the turnpike?

About seven miles an hour.

What is black and white and red all over?

A Dalmatian with a bad sunburn.

How did the shaggy dog feel when he
lost his flashlight?

Delighted.

How long are a shaggy dog's legs?

> *Long enough to reach the ground.*

•

Why did the shaggy dog jump off the
Empire State Building?

> *He wanted to make a hit on
> Broadway.*

If you take your shaggy dog downtown,
where should you leave him?

In a barking lot.

What happened to the shaggy dog that
fell into a lens-grinding machine?

He made a spectacle of himself.

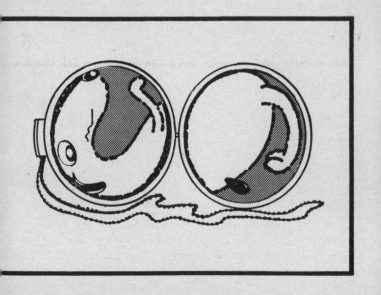

What is a baseball dog?

One that chases fowls.

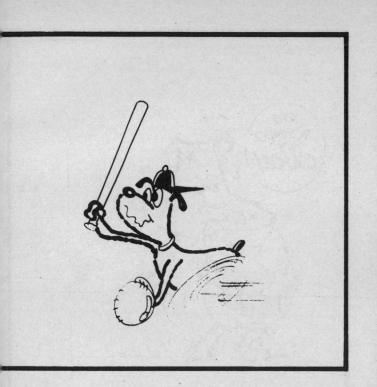

What should you do if you find an angry 500-pound shaggy dog in your kitchen?

Eat out.

What should you do if you find a
500-pound shaggy dog asleep on your
bed?

Sleep on the sofa.

●

What should you do if you find a
500-pound shaggy dog wearing your
favorite tie?

Go see a doctor. You have been
seeing entirely too many
500-pound shaggy dogs lately.

Why does a shaggy dog scratch himself?

He is the only one that knows where it itches.

What is the difference between a
barking shaggy dog and an umbrella?

The umbrella can be shut up.

●

What looks like a shaggy dog, sounds
like a shaggy dog, eats like a shaggy
dog, but isn't a shaggy dog?

A shaggy pup.

●

What would you call a nine-day-old
shaggy dog in Russia?

A puppy.

What is the difference between a
shaggy dog and a mailbox?

*If you don't know you must lose a
lot of mail.*

What did the shaggy dog do when he broke his toe?

He called a tow truck.

Why didn't the shaggy dog play cards
on his ocean cruise?

*Because the captain stood on the
deck.*

Why did the shaggy dog take a bag of oats to bed at night?

To feed his nightmares.

What does a shaggy dog become after it
is six years old?

Seven years old.

●

Why is a toothless shaggy dog like a
tree?

It has more bark than bite.

What is a shaggy dog who crosses the street twice in an hour?

A double crosser.

What did the shaggy dog get
when he
multiplied 497 by 684?

The wrong answer.

Why did the shaggy dog's owner think
his shaggy dog was a great
mathematician?

> *When he asked the dog what six
> minus six was, the dog said
> nothing.*

●

Which shaggy dog looks like a cat?

> *A police dog in disguise.*

●

What word did the shaggy dog always
pronounce incorrectly?

> *Incorrectly.*

Why did the shaggy dog mistake the dogcatcher for a grape?

He was color-blind.

Which side of a shaggy dog has the most
hair?

The outside, of course.

How do you keep a shaggy dog from
barking in your front yard?

Put him in your back yard.

●

What has 2,000 eyes and 4,000 feet?

A thousand shaggy dogs.

Eleven shaggy dogs shared one
umbrella, yet none got wet. How did
they manage?

It wasn't raining.

How did the shaggy dog make anti-freeze?

He stole her blanket.

Why did the shaggy dog go to the doctor after a tomato fell on his head?

The tomato was in a can.

Would you rather have a 300-pound dog chase you or a tiger?

> *I'd rather have him chase the tiger.*

●

Why was the mother flea so unhappy?

> *All her children had gone to the dogs.*

Why did the thoughtful father buy his six children a dachshund?

He wanted a dog they could all pet at once.

Why did the shaggy dog sleep on the chandelier?

He was a light sleeper.

What did the shaggy dog take when he was run down?

The license number of the car that hit him.

Why do shaggy dogs lie down?

They can't lie up.

Why doesn't a shaggy dog ever have a nose 12 inches long?

> *Because then it would be a foot.*

●

Where do you usually find shaggy dogs?

> *It all depends on where you lose them.*

If your shaggy dog jumped into a swimming pool, what is the first thing he would do?

Get wet.

Why is a shaggy dog so warm in summer?

He wears a coat and pants.

What did the shaggy dog do when the panhandler put the bite on him?

Bit him, naturally.

How did the shaggy dog make gold soup?

He put in 24 carrots.

When is a dog the most impolite?

When he points.

●

What did the shaggy dog say to the pig?

You are just a bore.

●

What flower did Lassie like best?

A collie flower.

When you catch your shaggy dog eating a dictionary, what should you do?

Take the words right out of his mouth.

How is a shaggy dog like a penny?

They both have a head and a tail.

What should you know before you teach
your shaggy dog a new trick?

*You should know more than your
dog.*

When do shaggy dogs have 16 legs?

When there are four of them.

•

Why is a shaggy dog like a baseball player?

He runs for home when he sees the catcher coming.

Why did the shaggy dog run in circles?

He was a watchdog and needed winding.

What is the shaggy dog's favorite tree?

The dogwood.

When is a shaggy dog most likely to
enter the house?

When the door is open.

●

How many hairs are in a shaggy dog's
tail?

None. They are all on the outside.

●

What dog can jump higher than a tree?

*Any dog can jump higher than a
tree. Trees don't jump.*

What did the shaggy dog use to make
his kite?

Flypaper.

Why did the police dog look like a
shaggy dog?

He was in the secret service.

Why do shaggy dogs turn around three
times before lying down?

One good turn deserves another.

What did the shaggy dog say to the
candle?

Are you going out tonight?

•

Why did the shaggy dog say meow?

*He was learning a foreign
language.*

Why did the shaggy dog jump up and down on the potato patch?

He hoped to raise mashed potatoes.

What time is it when five shaggy dogs
are chasing a cat down the street?

Five after one.

Why did the shaggy dog sleep so poorly?

> *By mistake he plugged his electric blanket into the toaster and kept popping out of bed all night.*

•

What is taller when it sits down than when it stands up?

> *A dog, shaggy or not.*

What happened when the shaggy dog swallowed a teaspoon?

He wasn't able to stir.

What eats dog food, lives in a doghouse, and is very dangerous?

A shaggy dog with a machine gun.

What should you do if you see a vicious shaggy dog?

Hope he doesn't see you.

Which shaggy dog can tell time?

A watchdog.

What did the shaggy dog do when a
man-eating tiger followed him?

> *Nothing. It was a man-eating
> tiger, not a shaggy-dog-eating
> one.*

How did the shaggy dog's owner know
his pet was angry about having soap
flakes for breakfast?

He foamed at the mouth.

How can you tell a shaggy dog from an elephant?

The elephant remembers.

●

What did the man do when his shaggy dog swallowed his pen?

Used a pencil instead.

How can you tell a shaggy dog from a tomato?

The tomato is red.

What place of business helps shaggy
dogs who have lost their tails?

A retail store.

What do shaggy dogs have that no other
animal has?

Puppies.

Why are shaggy dogs such poor
dancers?

They have two left feet.

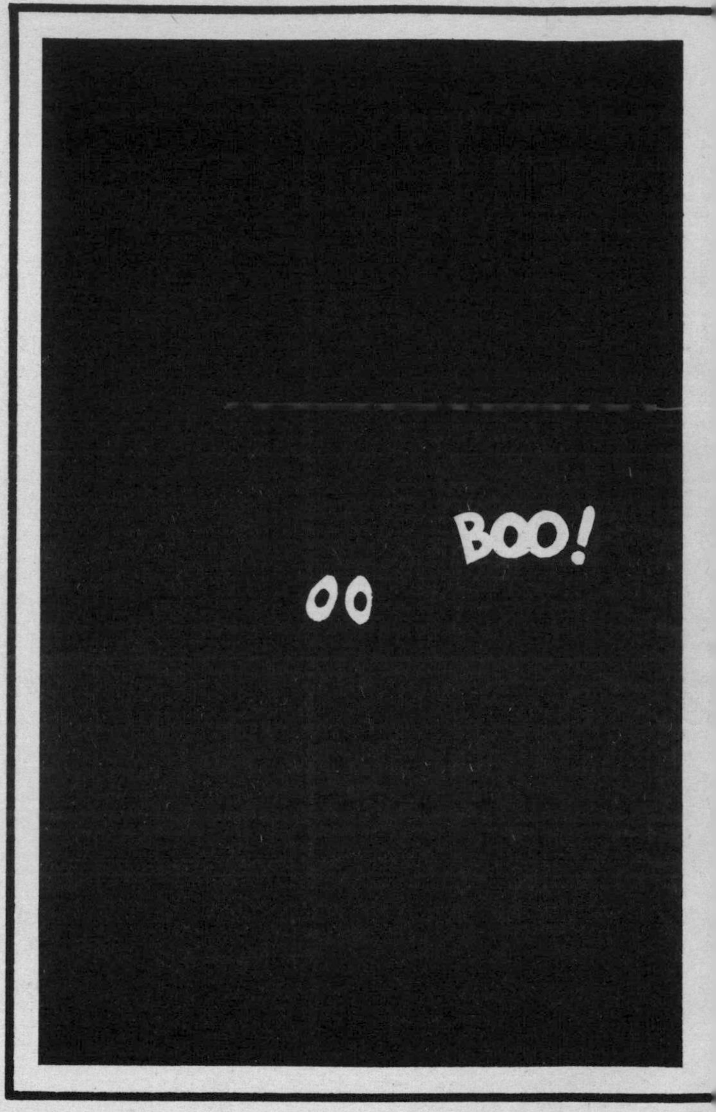
BOO!

Where was the shaggy dog when the lights went out?

In the dark.

How can you tell a shaggy dog from a
jar of peanut butter?

*The shaggy dog doesn't stick to
the roof of your mouth.*

●

What did the shaggy dog do at the flea
circus?

He stole the show.

Who gave the shaggy dog a black eye?

Nobody gave it to him. He had to fight for it.

How did the shaggy dog get into the locked cemetery at night?

He used a skeleton key.

Why did the shaggy dog have a gleam
in his eye?

> *Someone bumped his elbow while
> he was brushing his teeth.*

•

Why did the shaggy dog say he was an
actor?

> *His leg was in a cast.*

What did the shaggy dog do with the history professor?

They got together and talked over old times.

Why didn't the boy advertise in the paper when his shaggy dog was lost?

His dog never reads the paper.

●

What did the shaggy dog tell his owner when he saw the dogcatcher coming?

Nothing. Shaggy dogs don't talk.

How is a cowardly shaggy dog like a leaky faucet?

They both run.

●

What should you do with a blue shaggy dog?

Try to cheer him up.

What did the shaggy dog say when he chased his tail?

continued ▷

This is the end.